Practicing His Presence

Library of Spiritual Classics

This is Volume One of what will become a unique library of great Christian literature. It is a collection covering only one theme: how to experience Christ, in the depths. We are attempting to find, re-write and publish in modern English all outstanding literature written on this subject from the year 400 A.D. to 1800 A.D.

This book is a combination of three books. The first section is taken from excerpts of letters written at Dansalan, Lake Lanao, Philippine Islands by Frank Laubach to his father, 1930 through 1932, entitled *Letters by a Modern Mystic*. The second is from *The Game With Minutes*, also by Frank Laubach. The third is a modern rewrite of a book by Brother Lawrence, first printed in French in 1692, entitled *The Practice of the Presence of God*.

Additional volumes to the Library of Spiritual Classics are:

Practicing His Presence

Brother Lawrence
Frank Laubach

The SeedSowers

PO Box 3317
Jacksonville, FL 32206
www.seedsowers.com

Quotations from
Letters by a Modern Mystic
and
The Game With Minutes
are used by permission from
New Readers Press,
Syracuse, New York

Printed in the United States of America

Foreword

This book carries the testimony of two men's unique relationship with God . . . walking in the awareness of the presence of Christ . . . just as Christ walked about on earth, constantly aware of His Father.

Is such a relationship obtainable? Is it desirable? Is this experience central in the Christian Life??

The idea of living in the constant awareness of Christ has seemed so far-fetched that it has been generally discarded as hopelessly unobtainable. It really isn't! But if it *is* obtainable, why then has such a relationship to the Lord rarely been found among Christians during the last 2,000 years? The answer to that is very simple. Coming into a deep, constant awareness of Christ is a revelation unknown to most Christians. You do not seek after something that you do not know even exists.

Secondly, practicing a constant fellowship with

Christ has very rarely been experienced by any but a few men, isolated from others who shared such an experience.

So what has been missing? A corporate endeavor! A *group* of men and women together seeking to know nothing but Christ. This is what has been missing. *This,* the corporate venture, is what makes the difference . . . this is what takes away the difficulty. To put it more practically, when a group of people, *standing together with one another,* seek to live constantly in fellowship with Christ, suddenly the impossible is very obtainable.

This book was originally put together for just such a group of people. It was prepared for about 120 people who wanted to experience together what Brother Lawrence and Frank Laubach knew individually. The book is passed on to you with this word: The message of this book is for people in a practical experience of the *church*—the body of Christ. This wonderful relationship to Christ was *never* intended for the individual to seek alone nor to find alone. This relationship is for the church!! But when I say church, I speak of those few people who have had the privilege of living in the atmosphere of something called "church life."

You may wish to read the story of "The Early Church" to better appreciate what was lived out in the lives of first century believers. It is our goal to see that same experience known again, corporately, by the believers of our own day.

Gene Edwards

Contents

Introduction

There are two men in church history who have written very practically and simply on the subject of the practice of the presence of Christ. Both have a strong testimony to the reality of walking almost continually in the awareness of the presence of Christ. In our quest to know the Lord as well as He knows us, we can wisely turn to the experience of these two men. One of these men lived in the seventeenth century, the other in the twentieth.

The first of these two men is Brother Lawrence (Nicholas Herman) of France, who died in February of 1691. The second is Frank Laubach, who went to be with the Lord in June, 1970.

This book combines, under one cover, all that we have of Brother Lawrence's words on the subject of living in the presence of the Lord, and it also includes a condensation of two works by Frank Laubach on the same subject. (Frank Laubach's words are drawn from two small booklets, *Letters by a Modern Mystic* and *Games With Minutes.*)

We have very purposefully updated and rewritten the words of Brother Lawrence; the words of Frank Laubach have undergone only the slightest alterations.

Why rewrite the words of Brother Lawrence? Because most Christians who pick up his little book simply cannot understand many parts of it; the language is sometimes too archaic and the style too difficult to follow. We have therefore put his words and thoughts into more modern English. (The little booklet by him contained four conversations and sixteen letters. We have changed the "conversations" from third person to the first person.) You will still notice a flavor of his seventeenth century style even in this modified version; we have sought to leave in a slight hint of his own age.

As to the matter of condensing Frank Laubach's writing on the subject of Christ's presence, we wanted to omit from these letters discussions on other subjects and leave only that which is eternal. Perhaps by updating the words of Brother Lawrence he will be able to speak to the *next* century as well as he did to the *past* three centuries. And by condensing Frank Laubach's words, extracting the essence of his experience on this subject, perhaps he can speak to the Christian family with a message that will endure the centuries just as Brother Lawrence's words have.

As you read the writing of these two men, separated from one another by three hundred years,

x

you will catch the similarity of their hearts and experience. (Brother Lawrence wrote in the late 1600's. Brother Laubach wrote in the early 1930's; Laubach wrote first as one seeking; then as one who had found.) Let us look just a little closer at the lives of these two men, for our purpose in producing this little book is to stir and challenge you to their testimony: *living proof that it is possible to experience Christ continuously!*

The Life of Brother Lawrence

Little is known of Brother Lawrence. We will tell you what we know. He was born Nicholas Herman in French Lorraine in 1611. Born into poverty, at age eighteen he was converted to Christ. He later became a soldier, and then a footman (a servant who opens the carriage door, waits on tables, etc.).* Still later, in 1666, at the age of about 55, he entered a religious community called the Carmelites, located in Paris. He became a "Lay Brother" among these barefooted devotees to Christ. It was among them he took the name Brother Lawrence.

He spent twenty-five years† in this community, dying there at age eighty in 1691. During those years he served mostly in the hospital kitchen. He became known, within the community, and later beyond it, for his quiet and serene faith, and for his simple experience of "the presence of God."

---

*In about 1651, it appears, he had some kind of turning in his experience with Christ. From that time on he walked in the presence of God.

†Some believe, from evidence in his letters, he was a "Lay Brother" for 40 years rather than 25.

Eventually Brother Lawrence even received inquiries from people in other parts of France concerning how to have a similar reality in their own daily experience with Christ. Even church leaders sought him out for counsel and help.

Little is left to us of what he said. We have a few brief letters by him plus four recollections called "conversations" written by other people who recalled for us what he had said to them.

In 1692, a year after Brother Lawrence died, some of his letters were published. We decided to include in this book the preface to that first edition set in order by M. Beaufort, Grand Vicar to M. de Chalons (formerly Cardinal de Noailles) who recommended that these letters be published. This preface, now nearly three hundred years old, still reflects the simplicity of the man, and the esteem with which some held him.

Death has carried off many of the brothers of the order of the Carmelites Dechausses, in the last year. They died in the rare legacies of lives lived in virtue. Providence, it seems, has turned the eyes of men chiefly to the passing of Brother Lawrence.

Several people have seen a copy of one of Brother Lawrence's letters, and have wished to see more. In order to meet this request, care has been taken to collect as many letters as posssible which Brother Lawrence wrote with his own hand.

Every Christian will find much in these writings to edify him. Those in the thick of the world will learn from these letters how much they have deceived themselves, looking for peace and joy in the false glitter of things that can be seen . . . yet which are so temporary. And those who are seeking the Highest Good will gain strength from this book to persevere in the practice of virtue. All readers, whatever your occupation, will find profit in this book for in it you will meet a brother busy as you are in outward activity . . . but a brother who, in the middle of all his demanding tasks, had learned how to wed contemplation to activity. For the past forty years our brother has hardly ever turned from the "Presence of God."

During the nearly 300 years since these letters were first published, there have been unknown thousands, perhaps millions of copies of them printed. Now they come to you in modern language with the hope that the message that he so beautifully dealt with has only begun to be known.

The Life of Frank Laubach

Frank Laubach was born in the United States on September 2, 1884 . . . almost two hundred years after the death of Brother Lawrence. Forty-five years later Frank Laubach was serving as a missionary in the Philippines. Though he had done many commendable things by the time he was forty-five years of age, including a truly remarkable and faithful ministry among the Moslems in the southern Philippines, we would still have to confess he was a relatively obscure soldier of the cross.

It was at this time, at forty-five years of age, that Frank Laubach began the practice of abiding in the presence of Christ. It is so interesting to realize that forty years later, when Frank Laubach took what was for him a very short step out of time into eternity, he died — at the age of eighty-five — one of the most widely known and best loved men of the twentieth century.

To try to tell who Frank Laubach was or even to give a sketch of his life in a short space is simply impossible. From Signal Hill in the Philippines until his death at age eighty-five, on June 11, 1970, he lived one of the fullest lives ever lived by one of Christ's followers. He was one of the most traveled Christians of all ages; perhaps the most traveled man of modern times. He was known in virtually every land on earth. Countless honors were bestowed on him, though when once presented with a famous "Man of the Year" award he said humbly, "The Lord will not wish to count my trophies, but my scars."

He wrote over fifty books, several of them best sellers that had a world-wide influence. He was perhaps the greatest single educator of modern times. He has been referred to by many people as one of the most unique figures of this century. The accomplishments of his life are virtually endless. Nonetheless, the wellsprings of this incredible man's life can be traced back to that lovely, lonely little hill behind the shack where he lived on the island of Mindanao. Frank Laubach wrote down his experiences during these days in a series of letters to his father from which we have gleaned these writings. We sincerely hope that the words of Frank Laubach recorded here will become ageless and we prayerfully hope these words will endure as long as there are Christians left upon this earth to read them.

Practicing
His Presence

If there is any contribution that I have to make to the world that will live, surely it must be my experience of God on Signal Hill.
Frank Laubach, 1930

I
The Foretaste

January 3, 1930

To be able to look backward and say, "This has been the finest year of my life" — that is glorious! But anticipation! To be able to look ahead and say, "The present year can and shall be better!" — that is more glorious!

If we said such things about our achievements, we would be consummate egotists. But if we are speaking of God's kindness, and we speak truly, we are but grateful. And this is what I do witness. I have done nothing but open windows — *God has done all the rest.* There have been few if any conspicuous achievements. There has been a succession of marvelous experiences of the presence of God. I feel, as I look back over the year, that it would have been impossible to have held much more without breaking with sheer joy. It was the lonesomest year, in some ways the hardest year, of my life, but the most glorious, full of voices from heaven.

As for me, I resolved that I would succeed better this year with my experiment of filling *every minute full of the thought of God than I succeeded last year.*

January 20, 1930

Although I have been a minister and a missionary for fifteen years, I have not lived the entire day of every day, minute by minute to follow the will of God. Two years ago a profound dissatisfaction led me to begin trying to line up my actions with the will of God about every fifteen minutes or every half hour. Other people to whom I confessed this intention said it was impossible. I judge from what I have heard that few people are really trying even that. But this year I have started out to live all my waking moments in conscious listening to the inner voice, asking without ceasing, "What, Father, do you desire said? What, Father, do you desire this minute?"

It is clear that this is exactly what Jesus was doing all day every day.

January 26, 1930

For the past few days I have been experimenting in a more complete surrender than ever before. I am taking by deliberate act of will, enough time from each hour to give God much thought. Yesterday and today I have made a new adventure, which is not easy to express. I am feeling God in each movement, by an act of will — willing that He shall direct these fingers that now strike this typewriter — willing that He shall pour through my

2

steps as I walk — willing that He shall direct my words as I speak, and my very jaws as I eat!

You will object to this intense introspection. Do not try it, unless you feel dissatisfied with your own relationship with the Lord, but at least allow me to realize all the leadership of God I can. Paul speaks of our liberty in Christ. I am trying to be utterly free from everybody, free from my own self, but completely enslaved to the will of God every moment of this day.

We used to sing a song in the church in Benton which I like, but which I never really practiced until now. It runs:

> "Moment by moment I'm kept in His love;
> Moment by moment I've life from above;
> Looking to Jesus till glory doth shine;
> Moment by moment, O Lord, I am Thine."

It is exactly that "moment by moment," every waking moment, surrender, responsiveness, obedience, sensitiveness, pliability, "lost in His love," that I now have the mind-bent to explore with all my might, to respond to Jesus Christ as a violin responds to the bow of the master.

In defense of my opening my soul and laying it bare to the public gaze in this fashion, I may say that it seems to me that we really seldom do anybody much good excepting as we share the deepest experiences of our souls in this way. It is not the fashion to tell your inmost thoughts, but there are many wrong fashions, and concealment of the *best in us is wrong.* I disapprove of the usual practice of talking "small talk" whenever we meet, and holding a veil over our souls. If

3

we are so impoverished that we have nothing to reveal but small talk, then we need to struggle for more richness of soul. As for me, I am convinced that this spiritual pilgrimage which I am making is infinitely worthwhile, the most important thing I know of to talk about. And talk I shall while there is anybody to listen.

Outside the window, as I completed the last page, has been one of the most splendorous sunsets I have ever seen. And these words came singing through my soul, "Looking to Jesus 'till glory doth shine!" Open your soul and entertain the glory of God and after a while that glory will be reflected in the world about you and in the very clouds above your head.

II
Undiscovered Continents

January 29, 1930

I feel simply carried along each hour, doing my part in a plan which is far beyond myself. This sense of cooperation with God in little things is what so astonishes me, for I never have felt it this way before. I need something, and turn round to find it waiting for me. I must work, to be sure, but there is God working along with me. God takes care of all the rest. My part is to live this hour in continuous inner conversation with God and in perfect responsiveness to his will, to make this hour gloriously rich. This seems to be all I need think about.

March 1, 1930

The sense of being led by an unseen hand which takes mine while another hand reaches ahead and prepares the way, grows upon me daily. I do not need to strain at all to find opportunity. It piles in upon me as the waves roll over the beach, and yet there is time to do something about each opportunity.

Perhaps a man who has been an ordained minister since 1914 ought to be ashamed to confess that he never before felt the joy of complete hourly, minute by minute — now what shall I call it? — more than surrender. I had that before. More than listening to God. I tried that before. I cannot find the word that will mean to you or to me what I am now experiencing. It is a *will* act. I compel my mind to open straight out toward God. I wait and listen with determined sensitiveness. I fix my attention there, and sometimes it requires a long time early in the morning. I determine not to get out of bed until that mind set upon the Lord is settled. After a while, perhaps, it will become a habit, and the sense of effort will grow less.

But why do I constantly harp upon this inner experience? Because I feel convinced that for me, and for you who read, there lie ahead undiscovered continents of spiritual living compared with which we are infants in arms.

And I must witness that people outside are treating me differently. Obstacles which I once would have regarded as insurmountable are melting away like a mirage. People are becoming friendly who suspected or neglected me. I feel, I feel like one who has had his violin out of tune with the orchestra and at last is in harmony with the universe.

As for me, I never lived, I was half dead, I was a rotting tree, until I reached the place where I wholly, with utter honesty, resolved and then re-resolved that

I would find God's will and I would do that will though every fibre in me said no, and I would win the battle *in my thoughts*. It was as though some deep artesian well had been struck in my soul of souls and strength came forth. I do not claim success even for a day yet, not complete success all day, but some days are close to success, and every day is tingling with the joy of a glorious discovery. That thing is eternal. That thing is undefeatable. You and I shall soon blow away from our bodies. Money, praise, poverty, opposition, these make no difference, for they will all alike be forgotten in a thousand years, but this spirit which comes to a mind set upon continuous surrender, this spirit is timeless life.

March 9, 1930

For the first time in my life I know what I must do off in lonesome Lanao. I know why God left this aching void — for Himself to fill. Off on this mountain I must pursue this voyage of discovery in quest of God's will.

I must plunge into mighty experiments in intercessory prayer. I must confront these Moros with a divine love which will speak Christ to them.

III
Commitment
to an Experiment

March 15, 1930

This week a new, and to me marvelous experience, has come out of my loneliness. I have been so desperately lonesome that it was unbearable save by talking with God. And so every waking moment of the week I have been looking toward Him, with perhaps the exception of an hour or two.

Last Thursday night I was listening to a phonograph in Lumbatan and allowing my heart to commune when something broke within me, and I longed to lift my own will up and give it completely to God.

How infinitely richer this direct first hand grasping of God Himself is, than the old method which I used and recommended for years, the reading of endless devotional books. Almost it seems to me now that the very Bible cannot be read as a substitute for meeting God

9

soul to soul and face to face. And yet, how was this new closeness achieved? Ah, I know now that it was by cutting the very heart of my heart and by suffering. Somebody was telling me this week that nobody can make a violin speak the last depths of human longing until that soul has been made tender by some great anguish. I do not say it is the only way to the heart of God, but I must witness that it has opened an inner shrine for me which I never entered before.

March 23, 1930

One question now to be put to the test is this: Can we have that contact with God all the time? All the time awake, fall asleep in His arms, and awaken in His presence? Can we attain that? Can we do His will all the time? Can we think His thoughts all the time?

Or are there periods when business, and pleasures, and crowding companions must necessarily push God out of our thoughts? We cannot keep two things in mind at once. Indeed we cannot keep one thing in mind more than half a second. Our mind is a flowing something. It oscillates. Concentration is merely the continuous return to the same problem from a million angles. We do not think of one thing. We always think of the relationship of at least two things, and more often of three or more things simultaneously. So my problem is this: Can I bring the Lord back in my mind-flow every few seconds so that God shall always be in my mind?

I choose to make the rest of my life an experiment in answering this question.

Someone may be saying that this introspection and this struggle to achieve God-consciousness is abnormal and perilous. I am going to take the risks, for somebody ought to do it. If our religious premises are correct at all then this oneness with God is the most normal condition one can have. It is what made Christ, Christ. It is what St. Augustine meant when he said, "Thou hast made us for Thyself, and our souls are restless until they find their rest in Thee."

I do not invite anybody else to follow this arduous path. I wish many might. We need to know so much which one man alone cannot answer. For example:

"Can a laboring man successfully attain this continuous surrender to God? Can a man working at a machine pray for people all day long, talk with God all day long, and at the same time do his task efficiently?"

"Can a merchant do business, can an accountant keep books, ceaselessly surrendered to God?"

"Can a mother wash dishes, care for the babies, continuously talking to God?"

Is this obtainable?

Any hour of any day may be made perfect by merely choosing. It is perfect if one looks toward God that entire hour, waiting for His leadership all through the hour and trying hard to do every tiny thing exactly as God wishes it done, as perfectly as possible. No emotions are necessary. Just the doing of God's will perfectly makes the hour a perfect one.

IV
Failure and Success

April 18, 1930

I have tasted a thrill in fellowship with God which has made anything discordant with God disgusting. This afternoon the possession of God has caught me up with such sheer joy that I thought I never had known anything like it. God was so close and so amazingly lovely that I felt like melting all over with a strange blissful contentment. Having had this experience, which comes to me now several times a week, the thrill of filth repels me, for I know its power to drag me from God. And after an hour of close friendship with God my soul feels clean, as new fallen snow,

April 19, 1930

If this record of a soul's struggle to find God is to be complete it must not omit the story of difficulty and failure. This week, for example, has not been one of the finest in my life, though it has been above the average. I have undertaken something which, at my age at least, is hard, harder than I had anticipated. But I resolve not to give up the effort.

Yet strain does not seem to do good. At the moment I feel something "let go" inside, lo, God is here! It is a heart-melting "here-ness," a lovely whispering of father to child, and the reason I did not have it before, was because I had failed to let go.

Fellowship with God is something one dare not cover, for it smothers to death. It is like a tender infant or a delicate little plant, for long nurturing is the price of having it, while it vanishes in a second of time, the very moment indeed, one's eye ceases to be "single." One cannot worship God and Mammon for the reason that God slips out and is gone as soon as we try to seat some other unworthy affection beside Him. The other idol stays and God vanishes. Not because God is "a jealous God" but because sincerity and insincerity are contradictions and cannot exist at the same time in the same place.

The "experiment" is interesting, although I am not very successful, thus far. The thought of God slips out of my sight for I suppose two-thirds of every day, thus far. This morning I started out fresh, by finding a rich experience of God in the sunrise. Then I tried to let Him control my hands while I was shaving and dressing and eating breakfast. Now I am trying to let God control my hands as I pound the typewriter keys.

There is nothing that we can do excepting to throw ourselves open to God. There is, there must be, so much more in Him than He can give us, because we are so sleepy and because our capacity is so pitifully small. It ought to be tremendously helpful to be able to acquire the habit of reaching out strongly after God's thoughts, and to ask, "God, what have you to put into my mind now if only I can be large enough?" That waiting, eager attitude ought to give God the chance He needs. I am finding every day that the best of the five or six ways in which I try to keep contact with God is for me to wait for His thoughts, to ask Him to speak.

May 14, 1930

Oh, this thing of keeping in constant touch with God, of making Him the object of my thought and the companion of my conversations, is the most amazing thing I ever ran across. It is working. I cannot do it even half of a day — not yet, but I believe I shall be doing it some day for the entire day. It is a matter of acquiring a new habit of thought. Now I like the Lord's presence so much that when for a half hour or so He slips out of mind — as He does many times a day — I feel as though I had deserted Him, and as though I had lost something very precious in my life.

May 24, 1930

As I analyze myself I find several things happening to me as a result of these two months of strenuous effort to keep the Lord in mind every minute. This concentration upon God is strenuous, *but everything else has ceased to be so.* I think more clearly, I forget less frequently. Things which I did with a strain before, I now do

15

easily and with no effort whatever. I worry about nothing, and lose no sleep. I walk on air a good part of the time. Even the mirror reveals a new light in my eyes and face. I no longer feel in a hurry about anything. Everything goes right. Each minute I meet calmly as though it were not important. Nothing can go wrong excepting one thing. That is that God may slip from my mind if I do not keep on my guard. If He is there, the universe is with me. My task is simple and clear.

V
The Results . . .
So Far

June 1, 1930

Do you suppose that through all eternity the price we will need to pay for keeping God will be that we must endlessly be giving Him away?

From the point of view of experiment number one I should have to record a pretty high percentage of failure. But the other experiment — what happens when I do succeed — is so successful that it makes up for the failure of number one. God does work a change. The moment I turn to Him it is like turning on an electric current which I feel through my whole being. I find also that the effort does something to my mind which every mind needs to have done to it. I am given something that is difficult enough to keep my mind with a keen edge. The constant temptation of every man is to allow his mind to grow old and lose its edge. I feel that I am perhaps more lazy mentally than the average person, and I require the very mental discipline which this constant effort affords.

The most important discovery of my whole life is that one can take a little rough cabin and transform it into a palace just by flooding it with God. When one has spent many months in a little house like this in daily thoughts about God, the very entering of the house, the very sight of it as one approaches, starts associations which set the heart tingling and the mind flowing.

I am willing to confess that as yet I have not "striven unto blood" to win this battle. What I want to prove is that the thing can be done by all people under all conditions, but I have not proven it yet. This much I do see — what an incredibly high thing Jesus did.

A great lonesome hunger comes over me at this moment for someone who has passed through the same long, long channels of hope, and aspiration, and despair, and failure, to whom I can talk tonight. And yet — there is no such person. As we grow older all our paths diverge, and in all the world I suppose I could find nobody who could wholly understand me excepting God — and neither can you! Ah, God, what a new nearness this brings for Thee and me, to realize that Thou alone canst understand me, for Thou alone knowest all! Thou art no longer a stranger, God! Thou art the only being in the universe who is not partly a stranger! Thou art all the way inside with me — here. Ah, God, I mean to struggle tonight and tomorrow as never before, not once to dismiss Thee. For when I lose Thee for an hour I lose. The thing Thou wouldst do can only be done when Thou hast full sway all the time.

Last Monday was the most completely successful day of my life to date, so far as giving my day in complete and continuous surrender to God is concerned — though I shall hope for far better days — and I remember how as I looked at people with a love God gave, they looked back and acted as though they wanted to go with me. I felt then that for a day I saw a little of that marvelous pull that Jesus had as He walked along the road day after day "God-intoxicated" and radiant with the endless communion of His soul with God.

July 2, 1930

I am well aware of the probability of criticism because it is "mysticism" — as though any man could be a believer in Jesus without believing in "mysticism!" — or because many people think that the days of direct contact with God, or at least words from God, stopped with the closing of the New Testament. But then what a stupid world this would be if one never did anything different for fear of criticism!

August 21, 1930

I shall be forty-six in two weeks. I no longer have the sense that life is all before me, as I had a few years ago. Some of it is behind — and a miserable poor part it is, so far below what I had dreamed that I dare not even think of it. Nor dare I think much of the future. This present, if it is full of God, is the only refuge I have from poisonous disappointment and even almost rebellion against God.

Here I was, engaging in the most glorious action of all human and of all superhuman life — I was communing with the very God of the universe Himself. He was showing me His very heart, even the angels can do no more than this. I forgot that my being choked down against the bottom of an ocean like an octopus, and like an octopus in disposition, too, makes no difference at all. A prison or a dungeon makes no difference if one is with God. We preach and profess that as true, and it is true, but upon my word I do not see many people who seem to have experienced it.

VI
When He Gave
His Presence

September 2, 1930

Tip and I and God were together on Signal Hill. Oh, God, let me put on paper the glory that was there. I suppose it was because I was trying to make this first day of my forty-sixth year high. And that, I suppose, is why all of us have some high days and some low ones. God is always awaiting the chance to give us high days. We so seldom are in deep earnest about giving Him His chance.

September 21, 1930

Our search for God through narrow straits has brought a sudden revelation, like an explorer who has just come out upon a limitless sea. It is not any particularly new idea but a new feeling, which came almost of itself. Today God seems to me to be just behind everything. I feel Him there. He is just under my hand, just under the typewriter, just behind this desk, just inside the file, just inside the camera.

One of these Moro fairy tales has the fairies standing behind every rock looking at the hero. That is how I feel about God today. Of course this is only a way of symbolizing the truth that God is invisible and that He is everywhere. I cannot imagine seeing the invisible, but I can imagine God hiding Himself behind everything in sight.

For a lonesome man there is something infinitely homey and comforting in feeling God so close, so everywhere!

It is difficult to convey to another the joy of having broken into the new sea of realizing God's "hereness." It seemed so wonderfully true that just the privilege of fellowship with God is infinitely more than anything God could give. When He gives Himself He is giving more than anything else in the universe.

September 22, 1930

It is our duty to live in the beauty of the presence of God on some mount of transfiguration until we become white with Christ. After all, the deepest truth is that the Christ-like life is glorious, undefeatably glorious. There is no defeat unless one loses God, and then all is defeat, though it be housed in castles and buried in fortunes.

October 12, 1930

How I wish, wish, wish that a dozen or more persons who are trying to hold God endlessly in mind would all write their experiences so that each would know what the other was finding as a result! The results, I think, would astound the world. At least the results of my own effort are astounding to me.

Worries have faded away like ugly clouds and my soul rests in the sunshine of perpetual peace. I can lie down anywhere in this universe bathed around by my own Father's Spirit. The very universe has come to seem so homey! I know only a little more about it than before, but that little is all! It is vibrant with the electric ecstacy of God! I know what it means to be "God-intoxicated."

If our destiny is to grow on and on and on, into some far more beautiful creatures than we are now, that means that we need to have the shells broken quite frequently so that we can grow.

I wish to tell all the world that it needs a better way, that God on Signal Hill satisfies, and sends through me a flow of glory which makes me sure that this is the pathway of true intuition.

February 25, 1931

This is the best way to act: talk a great deal to the Lord.

March 3, 1931

Oh, if we only let God have His full chance He will break our heart with the glory of His revelation. It is my business to look into the very face of God until I ache with bliss. That is how I feel this morning after two hours with God. And now on this "mount of transfiguration" I do not ever want to leave.

April 5, 1931

Choosing Christ brings mystery, rejecting Him brings despair.

VII
Heavenly Life

September 18, 1931

I choose to look at people through God, using God as my glasses, colored with His love for them.

Last year, as you know, I decided to try to keep the Lord in mind all the time. That was rather easy for a lonesome man in a strange land. It has always been easier for the shepherds, and the monks, and the anchorites than for people surrounded by crowds.

But today it is an altogether different thing. I am no longer lonesome. The hours of the day from dawn to bedtime are spent in the presence of others. Either this new situation will crowd God out or I must take Him into it all. I must learn a continuous silent conversation of heart to heart speaking with God while looking into other eyes and listening to other voices.

I cannot get God by holding Him off at arm's length like a photograph, but by leaning forward intently as one would respond to one's lover. Love so insatiable as the love of God can never be satisfied until we respond to the limit.

September 28, 1931

When one has struck some wonderful blessing that all mankind has a right to know about, no custom or false modesty should prevent him from telling it, even though it may mean the unbarring of his soul to the public gaze.

I have found such a way of life. I ask nobody else to live it, or even to try it. I only witness that it is wonderful, it is indeed heaven on earth. And it is very simple, so simple that any child could practice it.

This simple practice requires only a gentle pressure of the will, not more than a person can exert easily. It grows easier as the habit becomes fixed.

Yet it transforms life into heaven. Everybody takes on a new richness, and all the world seems tinted with glory. I do not, of course, know what others think of me, but the joy which I have within cannot be described. If there never were any other reward than that, it would more than justify the practice to me.

October 11, 1931

There are three questions which we may ask: "Do you believe in God?" That is not getting very far. "The devils believe and tremble." Second, "Are you acquainted with God?" We are acquainted with people with whom we have had some business dealings. Third,

26

"Is God your friend?" or putting this another way, "Do you love God?"

It is this third stage that is really vital. How is it to be achieved? Precisely as any friendship is achieved. By doing things together. The depth and intensity of the friendship will depend upon the variety and extent of the things we do and enjoy together. Will the friendship be constant? That again depends upon the permanence of our common interests, and upon whether or not our interests grow into ever widening circles, so that we do not stagnate. The highest friendship demands growth. "It must be progressive as life itself is progressive." Friends must walk together; they cannot long stand still together, for that means death to friendship and to life.

Friendship with God is the friendship of child with parent. As an ideal son grows daily into a closer relationship with his father, so we may grow into closer love with God by widening into His interests, and thinking His thoughts and sharing His enterprises.

Far more than any other device of God to create love was the cross where the lovingest person the world has known hangs loving through all His pain. That cross has become the symbol of love for a third of the world because it touches the deepest depths of human love.

January 2, 1932

I resolve to accept each situation of this year as God's layout for that hour, and never to lament that it is a very commonplace or disappointing task. One can pour something divine into every situation.

One of the mental characteristics against which I have rebelled most is the frequency of my "blank spells" when I cannot think of anything worth writing, and sometimes cannot remember names. Henceforth I resolve to regard these as God's signal that I am to stop and listen. Sometimes you want to talk to your son, and sometimes you want to hold him tight in silence. God is that way with us, He wants to hold us still with Him in silence.

Here is something we can share with all the people in the world. They cannot all be brilliant or rich or beautiful. They cannot all even dream beautiful dreams like God gives some of us. They cannot all enjoy music. Their hearts do not all burn with love. But everybody can learn to hold God. And when God is ready to speak, the fresh thoughts of heaven will flow in like a crystal spring. Everybody rests at the end of the day, what a gain if everybody could rest in the waiting arms of the Father, and listen until He whispers.

VIII
Practical Help

We shall not become like Christ until we give Him more time.

A teachers' college requires students to attend classes for twenty-five hours a week for three years. Could it prepare competent teachers or a law school prepare competent lawyers if they studied only ten minutes a week? Neither can Christ, and He never pretended that He could. To His disciples He said: "Come with me, walk with me, eat and sleep with me, twenty-four hours a day for three years." That was their college course. "He chose them," the Bible says, "that they might be with Him," 168 hours a week!

All who have tried that kind of abiding for a month know the power of it — it is like being born again from center to circumference. It absolutely changes every person who does it. How can a man or woman do this?

Indeed, unless we "turn and become like children" we cannot succeed.

Try to call Christ to mind at least one second of each minute. You do not need to forget other things nor stop your work, but invite Him to share everything you do or say or think. There are those who have experimented until they have found ways to let Him share every minute that they are awake. In fact, it is no harder to learn this new habit than to learn the touch system in typing, and in time a large part of the day's minutes are given over to the Lord with as little effort as an expert needs to type a letter. This practicing the presence of Christ takes all our time, yet does not take from our work. It takes Christ into our enterprises and makes them more successful.

Practicing the presence of God is not on trial. It has already been proven by countless saints. Indeed, the spiritual giants of all ages have known it. The results of this effort begin to show clearly in a month. They grow rich after six months, and glorious after ten years. This is the secret of the great saints of all ages. "Pray without ceasing," said Paul, "in everything make your wants known unto God." "As many as are *led* by the spirit of God, these are the sons of God."

Nobody is wholly satisfied with himself. Our lives are made up of lights and shadows, of some good days and many unsatisfactory days. We have learned that the good days and hours come when we are very close to Christ. Clearly, then, the way to more such days and hours is to take Him into everything we do or say or think.

Experience has told us that good resolutions are not enough. We need to discipline our lives to an ordered regime. So many of us have found the idea of turning to Christ once every minute to be enormously helpful. It is a practice as old as Enoch, who "walked with God." It is a way of living which nearly everybody knows and nearly everybody has ignored. Some will at once recognize it as a fresh approach to Brother Lawrence's "Practicing the Presence of God." It is a delightful experience and an exhilarating spiritual exercise; but we soon discover that it is far more than even that. Some people have compared it to getting out of a dark prison and beginning to *live*. We still see the same world, yet it is not the same, for it has a new, glorious color and a far deeper meaning.

You will find this just as easy and just as hard as forming any other habit. You have hitherto thought of the Lord for only a few seconds or minutes a week, and He was out of your mind the rest of the time. Now you are attempting, like Brother Lawrence, to have the Lord in mind each minute you are awake. Such drastic change in habit requires a real effort *at the beginning*.

How To Begin

Select a favorable hour, an easy, uncomplicated hour. See how many minutes of the hour you can remember, or touch, Christ at least once each minute; that is to say, bring Him to mind at least one second out of every sixty. You will not do so well at first but keep trying, for it constantly becomes easier, and after a while is almost automatic. When you begin to try this you discover that

31

spiritually you are still a very weak infant. A babe in the crib seizes upon everything at hand to pull himself to his feet, wobbles for a few seconds and falls exhausted. Then he tries again, each time standing a little longer than before.

Suppose you have enjoyed a good time in the presence of the Lord, and then you find yourself with a group of friends engaged in ordinary conversation. Can you recall the Lord at least once every minute? This is hard, but here are some helps. Keep humming to yourself (inaudibly) a favorite hymn - For example, "Have Thine Own Way, Lord, Have Thine Own Way." Keep whispering inside, "Lord, You are my life," or "You are my thought."

Here are a few aids which have proven helpful:

When at the table remember Jesus' words, "Eat this in remembrance of Me." This can be applied to ordinary meals so that every mouthful is His "body broken for you."

When reading, keep a running conversation with Him about the pages you are reading.

If you lean back to consider some problem, how can you remember the Lord? By forming a new habit! All thought employs silent words and is really conversation with your inner self. Instead of talking to yourself, form the habit of talking to Christ. Some of us who have done this find it so much better that we never want the other way again. No practice we have ever found has held the mind as much as this: making all thought a conversation with the Lord. When evil thoughts of any kind come, say, "Lord, these thoughts are not fit to discuss with you. Lord, you do the thinking. Renew my mind by your presence."

When you are strolling out of doors alone, you can recall the Lord at least once every minute with no effort. If you wander to a place where you can talk aloud without being overheard, you may speak to the invisible Companion inside you. Ask Him what is most on His heart and then answer back aloud with your voice what you believe God replies to you. Of course, we are not always sure whether we have guessed His answer correctly, but it is surprising how much of the time we are very certain. It really is not necessary to be sure that our answer is right, for the answer is not the great thing -- He is! God is infinitely more important than His advice or His gifts; indeed, He, Himself, is the great gift. The most precious privilege in talking with Christ is this intimacy which we can have with Him. We may have a glorious succession of heavenly minutes. How foolish we are to lose life's most poignant joy, seeing it may be had while taking a walk alone! But the most wonderful discovery of all is, to use the words of Paul, "Christ liveth in me." He dwells in us, walks in our minds, reaches out through our hands, speaks with our voices, if we respond to His every whisper.

Make sure that your last thoughts are of Christ as you are falling asleep at night. Continue to whisper any words of endearment your heart suggests. If all day long you have been walking with Him, you will find Him the dear companion of your dreams. Sometimes after such a day, we have fallen asleep with our pillows wet from tears of joy, feeling His tender touch on our foreheads. Usually, you will feel no deep emotion, but will always have a "peace that passeth all understanding." This is the end of a perfect day.

On waking in the morning, you may ask, "Now, Lord, shall we get up?" Some of us whisper to Him our every thought about washing and dressing in the morning.

Men have found they can keep the Lord in mind while engaged in all types of work, mental or manual, and find that they are happier and get better results. Those who endure the most intolerable ordeals gain new strength when they realize that their Unseen Comrade is by their side. (To be sure, no man whose business is harmful or whose methods are dishonest, can expect God's partnership.) The carpenter can do better work if he talks quietly to God about each task, as Jesus surely did when He was a carpenter.

There are women who cultivate Christ's companionship while cooking, washing dishes, sweeping, sewing, and caring for children. Aids which they find helpful are: whisper to the Lord about each small matter, knowing that He loves to help. Hum or sing a favorite hymn.

Students can enjoy the presence of the Lord even when taking an examination. Say, "Father, keep my mind clear, and help me remember all I have learned. How shall *we* answer this next question?" He will not tell you what you have never studied, but He does sharpen your memory and take away your stage fright when you ask Him.

Troubles and pain come to those who practice

God's presence, as they came to Jesus, but these seem not so important as compared to their new joyous experience. If we have spent our days with Him, we find that when earthquakes, fires, famines or other catastrophes threaten us, we are not terrified any more than Paul was in time of shipwreck. "Perfect love casteth out fear."

Some Prices We Must Pay

The first price is pressure of our wills, gentle but constant. But what prize is ever won without effort?

The second price is perseverance. Poor results at the outset are not the slightest reason for discouragement; everybody has this experience for a long while. Each week grows better and requires less strain.

The third price is perfect surrender. We lose Christ's presence the moment our wills rebel. If we try to keep even a remote corner of life for self or evil, and refuse to let the Lord rule us wholly, that small worm will spoil the entire fruit. We must be utterly sincere.

The fourth price is to be often in a group. We need the stimulus of believers who pursue what we pursue, the presence of Christ.

What We Gain

You may not win all your minutes to Christ, or even half, but you do win a richer life. There are no losers excepting those who quit.

We develop what Thomas a Kempis calls a "familiar friendship with Jesus." Our unseen Friend becomes dearer, closer and more wonderful every day

35

until at last we know Him as "Jesus, lover of my soul," not only in song *but in blissful experience.* Doubts vanish; we are more sure of Him being with us than of anybody else. This warm, ardent friendship ripens rapidly, and it keeps on growing richer and more radiant every month.

We gain purity of thought, because when we are maintaining the presence of Christ, our minds are pure as a mountain stream every moment.

All day long we are contented, whatever our lot may be, for He is with us. "When Jesus goes with me, I'll go anywhere."

It becomes easy to tell others about Christ because our minds are flooded with Him. "Out of the fullness of the heart the mouth speaks."

It Is For Anybody

The notion that religion is dull, stupid and sleepy is abhorrent to God, for He has created infinite variety and He loves to surprise us. If you are weary of some sleepy form of devotion, probably God is as weary of it as you are. Shake out of it, and approach Him in one of the countless fresh directions.

Humble folk often believe that walking with God is above their heads, or that they may "lose a good time" if they share all their joys with Christ. What tragic misunderstanding to regard Him as a killer of happiness! A chorus of joyous voices round the world fairly sing that spending their hours with the Lord is the most thrilling joy ever known, and that beside it a ball game or a horse race is stupid. Spending time with the Lord is not a grim duty. And if you should forget Him for minutes or even days, *do not groan or repent,* but begin anew with a smile. Every minute can be a fresh beginning.

Lord I am yours, dryness does not matter nor affect me! Brother Lawrence

IX
A Simple Testimony

Conversation with a Friend August 3, 1666
God did me a glorious favor in bringing me to a conversion at the age of eighteen.

In the winter I saw a tree stripped of its leaves and I knew that within a little time the leaves would be renewed, and that afterwards the flowers and the fruit would appear. From this I received a high view of the power and providence of God which has never since departed from my soul. The view I grasped that day set me completely loose from the world and kindled in me such a love for God that I cannot tell whether it has increased during the more than forty years since that time.

I was a footman to M. Fieubert, the treasurer, but I am a very awkward fellow and seemed to break everything.

I decided, instead of continuing as a footman, to be

received into a monastery. I thought that perhaps there I would be made, in some way, to suffer for my awkwardness and for all the faults I had committed. I decided to sacrifice my life with all its pleasures to God. But He greatly disappointed me in this idea, for I have met with nothing but satisfaction in giving my life over to Him.

I have found that we can establish ourselves in a sense of the presence of God by continually talking with Him. It is simply a shameful thing to quit conversing with Him to think of trifles and foolish things. We should feed and nourish our souls with high notions of God which will yield great joy.

We ought to quicken, that is, enliven our faith. It is lamentable that we have so little faith. Men amuse themselves with trivial devotions which change daily instead of making faith in God the rule of their conduct. The way of faith is the spirit of the church and it is sufficient to bring us to a very high degree of perfection.

We ought to give ourselves up to God in things that are temporal as well as in things that are spiritual. We should seek our satisfaction only in fulfilling His will. If He leads us into suffering or if He leads us into comfort, our satisfaction should still only be for the fulfilling of His will, for both suffering and comfort are the same to a soul truly resigned to Him.

There are times in prayer when God tries our love for Him. In these times of dryness and unclearness which bother our souls, there needs to be fidelity to Him. This is the time for us to make an effectual act of resignation. This will oftentimes increase our spiritual advancement.

Just say, "Lord I am yours, dryness does not matter nor affect me!"

To arrive at the resignation God requires, we should watch attentively over all our passions. These passions mingle as much in spiritual things as in things of a more gross nature. God will give light about these passions to anyone who truly desires to serve Him.

If that is your desire, to sincerely serve God, you may feel free to come to me as often as you please without fear of being troublesome. But if you do not have this as your sincere desire there is no necessity of your visiting with me again.

X
The Moment
That Changed Everything

I have always been governed by love without selfish views, and have resolved to make the love of God the end of all my actions. I have been well satisfied with this single motive. I am pleased when I can take a straw from the ground simply for the love of God, seeking Him only and nothing else — not even seeking His gifts.

I was long troubled by the belief that perhaps I would be damned. All the men in the world could not have persuaded me to the contrary. Then I reasoned with myself: I have engaged in a religious life only for the love of God; I have endeavored to act only for Him; whatever becomes of me, whether I be lost or saved, I will always continue to act purely for the love of God. I shall have this good at least, that till death I shall have done all that is in me to love God. That troubled state of mind had been with me for years. I had suffered much

45

during that time; but since the time I saw this trouble arose from lack of faith, I have passed my life in perfect liberty and continual joy. I even placed my sins between myself and the Lord to tell Him that I did not deserve His favors, but He continued to bestow His favors upon me, in abundance, anyway!

In order to first form the habit of conversing with God continually and of referring all that we do to Him, we must first apply ourselves to Him with diligence. After a little such care we shall find His love inwardly excites us to His presence without any difficulty.

I expect that, after the pleasant days that God has given me, I will have my turn of pain and suffering. But I am not uneasy about this, knowing very well that since I can do nothing of myself, God will not fail to give me the strength to bear it.

On some occasions when it has been my opportunity to exercise some virtue, I have turned to God confessing, "Lord I cannot do this unless You enable me." I then received strength that was more than sufficient.

When I fail in my duty I simply admit my faults, saying to God, "I shall never do otherwise if You leave me to myself. It is You who must stop my falling and it is You who must amend that which is amiss." After such praying I allow myself no further uneasiness about my faults.

In all things we should act toward God with the greatest simplicity, speaking to Him frankly and plainly and imploring His assistance in our affairs just as they happen. God never fails to grant that assistance, as has often been my experience.

Recently I went to Burgundy to buy the wine provisions for the society which I have joined. This was a very unwelcome task for me. I have no natural business ability and, being lame, I cannot get around the boat except by rolling myself over the casks. Nonetheless, this matter gave me no uneasiness, nor did the purchase of wine. I told the Lord that it was His business that I was about. Afterwards, I found the whole thing well performed.

And so it is the same in the kitchen (a place to which I have a great natural aversion). I have accustomed myself to doing everything there for the love of God. On all occasions, with prayer, I have found His grace to do my work well, and I have found it easy during the fifteen years in which I have been employed here.

I am very well pleased with the post that I am now in but I am as ready to quit it as I was my former occupation, since in every condition I please myself by doing little things for the love of God.

My set times of prayer are not different from other times of the day. Although I do retire to pray (because it is the direction of my superior) I do not need such retirement nor do I ask for it because my greatest business does not divert me from God.

I am aware of my obligations to love God in all things and as I endeavor to do so I have no need of a director to advise me although I need a confessor to absolve me. I am keenly aware of my faults, but I am not discouraged by them. When I have confessed my faults to the Lord, I peacefully resume my usual practice of love and adoration to Him.

When I have a troubled mind I do not consult anyone. But knowing, by the light of faith, that God is with me in all things, I am content with directing all of my actions to Him. In other words, I carry out my actions with the desire to please the Lord and then let all else come as it will.

Our useless thoughts spoil everything. They are where mischief begins. We ought to reject such thoughts as soon as we perceive their impertinence to the matter at hand. We ought to reject them and return to our communion with God.

In the beginning I often passed my appointed time for prayer in simply rejecting wandering thoughts and then falling back into them. I also meditated for some time, but afterward ceased from that exercise — how exactly I cannot account for. I have never been able to regulate my devotion by certain methods, as some do.

All bodily mortification and other exercises are useless except as they serve to arrive at union with God by love. I have well considered this and found that the shortest way to God is to go straight to Him by a continual exercise of love and doing all things for His sake.

We ought to make a great difference between the acts of the understanding and those of the will. Acts in response to our own mental understanding are of comparatively little value. Action we take in response to the deep impressions of our heart are of all value. Our only business is to love and delight ourselves in God.

All kinds of mortification, no matter what they are,

if they are void of the love of God, cannot erase a single sin. We ought, without any anxiety, to expect the pardon of our sins from the blood of the Lord Jesus Christ; our only endeavor should be to love Him with all our hearts. God seems to have granted the greatest favor to the greatest sinners, as more signal monuments of His mercy.

The greatest pains or pleasures of this world are not to be compared with what I have experienced of both pain and pleasure in a spiritual state. Therefore, I am careful for nothing and fear nothing, desiring only one thing of God — that I might not offend Him.

I have no scruples; for when I fail in my duty I readily acknowledge it saying, ''I am used to doing so; I shall never do otherwise if I am left to myself.'' If I do not fail, then I give God thanks, acknowledging that the strength comes from Him.

XI
A New View of Him

The foundation of spiritual life, for me, has been a high image of God and a high esteem of God — both of which I arrive at by faith.

Once this has been well conceived I have had no other care but to faithfully reject every other thought in order to perform all my actions for the love of God. If sometimes I have not thought of God for a good while, I do not become disquieted because of it. But, after having acknowledged my failure to God, I return to Him with even greater trust since I was so miserable in having forgotten Him.

The simple trust we put in God honors Him much and draws down His great graces. It is impossible not only that God should deceive but also that He should let a soul which is perfectly resigned to Him suffer long, a soul that has resolved to endure everything for the Lord's sake.

I have very often experienced the ready help of divine grace upon all occasions. When I have business to do, I do not think about it beforehand. When the time comes to do it, I see in God as clearly as in a mirror all that is needed for me to do.

When outward business diverts me a while from the thought of God, a fresh remembrance coming from Him invests itself into my soul, and I am so inflamed and transported that it is sometimes difficult for me to contain myself.

I am more united to God in my outward employments than when I leave them for devotion and retirement.

I expect hereafter some great pain both of body and mind. But the worst that could happen to me would be to lose that sense of God which I have enjoyed so long. Nonetheless, the goodness of God assures me that He will not forsake me utterly; He will give me strength to bear whatever evil that He permits to happen to me. Therefore, I fear nothing and I have no reason to consult with anyone else about my state. When I have attempted to consult with others about my situation I have always come away more perplexed. I am conscious of my readiness to lay down my life for the love of God and I have no apprehension of danger. Perfect resignation to God is a sure way to heaven, a way in which I have always had sufficient light for my conduct.

In the beginning of the spiritual life we ought to be faithful in doing our duty and also in denying ourselves. After that, unspeakable pleasures will follow. When difficulties arise we need only have recourse to Jesus

Christ and beg His grace. With that everything becomes easy.

Many do not advance in Christian progress because they stick to penances and to particular exercises while they neglect the love of God — and the love of God is the end. This is plainly revealed by their works, and is the reason we see so little solid virtue.

We need neither art nor science for going to God. All we need is a heart resolutely determined to apply itself to nothing but Him, for His sake, and to love Him only.

XII
The Most Excellent Method

Let me just comment with an open heart about my manner of going to God. All things hinge upon your hearty renunciation of everything which you are aware does not lead to God. You need to accustom yourself to continual conversation with Him — a conversation which is free and simple. We need to recognize that God is always intimately present with us and address Him every moment. In things that are doubtful we need to ask His assistance to know His will. And the things we plainly see He requires of us, we should rightly perform. As we go about this pursuit we should simply offer all things to Him before we do them and give Him thanks when we have finished.

In your conversation with God, be also employed in praising Him, adoring Him, and loving Him incessantly, doing all of these things because of His infinite goodness and His perfection.

We ought not to be discouraged on account of our sins; rather, simply pray for the Lord's grace with perfect confidence, relying upon the infinite mercies of the Lord Jesus Christ. God has never failed offering us His grace at each action. I can distinctly perceive that grace, and I am never without a sense of that grace unless it is when my thoughts have wandered from a sense of God's presence or I have forgotten to ask the Lord for His assistance.

God always gives us light in our doubt when we have no other design except to please Him.

Our sanctification does not depend upon changing our works, but in doing for God's sake all those things which we commonly do for our own. It is lamentable to see how many people mistake the means for the end, becoming addicted to certain of their works. They do not perform these works perfectly because of their human selfish aim.

The most excellent method I have found of going to God is that of doing common business without any view to pleasing men, and as far as I am capable, doing it purely for the love of God.

It is a great delusion to think that the time of prayer ought to be different from other times. We are strictly obliged to adhere to God in the time of action, just as we are to adhere to prayer during the season of prayer.

My prayers are nothing other than a sense of the presence of God. My soul is simply insensible, at that time, to anything but divine love. When the appointed time of prayer has passed, I find no difference because

I still continue with God, praising and blessing Him with all my might, so that I might pass my life in continual joy. Yet I hope that God will give me more suffering when I grow stronger.

We ought not to be weary in doing little things for the love of God. For God does not regard the greatness of the work but the love with which it is performed. We should not wonder if in the beginning we fail in our endeavor to pursue this manner of life. In the end, we shall gain a habit which will naturally produce its acts in us, acts done without any care but rather with exceeding great delight.

The whole substance of religion is simply faith, hope and love. By practicing these we become united to the will of God. Everything else is immaterial and is simply a means of arriving at our end — to be swallowed up in our unity to the will of God through faith and love.

All things are possible to him who believes; they are less difficult to him who hopes; they are easier to him who loves, and they are easier still to him who perseveres in the practice of all three of these virtues.

We ought to purpose ourselves towards this end: to become in this life the most perfect worshipper of God we can possibly be (since that is what we hope to be throughout all eternity).

When we enter into the spiritual life, we should consider and examine what we are to the very bottom. We would then find ourselves worthy of all contempt and not deserving the name Christian. We are subject to all kinds of misery and numberless accidents which trouble us and cause perpetual vicissitudes in our health, our humor, and our disposition, both within and without. Therefore, we should not wonder that troubles, temptations, oppositions and contradictions happen to us from men. On the contrary, we ought to submit ourselves to these and bear them as long as God pleases, for they are highly advantageous to us.

The greater the perfection you aspire to have, the more dependent you must become upon divine grace.

XIII
Nothing But Him

I have read many accounts in different books on how to go to God and how to practice the spiritual life. It seems these methods serve more to puzzle me than to help, for what I sought after was simply how to become wholly God's. So I resolved to give all for ALL. Then I gave myself wholly to God; I renounced everything that was not His. I did this to deal with my sins, and because of my love for Him. *I began to live as if there were nothing, absolutely nothing but Him.* So upon this earth I began to seek to live as though there were only the Lord and me in the whole world.

Sometimes I would simply consider myself before Him: He the judge, I the criminal. But at other times I beheld Him as being in my heart — as my Father, as my God. I worshipped Him as often as I could. I kept my mind *in* His holy presence. I recalled His presence as often as I found my mind wandering from Him. I found this to be a very difficult exercise! Yet I continued despite the difficulties I encountered. I did not allow myself to become upset when my mind wandered.

I made it my business to be in the Lord's presence just as much throughout the day as I did when I came to my appointed time of prayer. I drove anything from my mind that was capable of interrupting my thought of God. I did this all the time, every hour, every minute, even in the height of my daily business.

I have been making this my common practice ever since I entered monastic life. Certainly I have done this imperfectly, yet I have found a great advantage in this pursuit. Because of my failures I know all glory must be imparted solely to the mercy and goodness of God. We can do nothing without Him . . . and I can do still less than anyone else. Nonetheless, when we are faithful to keep ourselves in His holy presence and to set His face always before us, there is a good result. We are kept from offending Him and from willfully doing those things which displease Him. But even more, such an exercise begets in us a holy freedom and a familiarity with God. We ask, and ask successfully, for the grace we stand in need of. In short, by often repeating these acts they become habit. The presence of God becomes natural to us.

Give Him thanks, if you please, with me, for His great goodness toward me. I can never sufficiently marvel at the many favors He has done for so miserable a sinner as I am.

May all things praise Him.

Amen.

XIV
A Friend's Testimony

November 3, 1685

I would like to take this opportunity to communicate to you the sentiments of one of the people here in our Society concerning the wonderful effects and continual strength which he receives from the presence of God. We can both profit from it.

He has been in religion for forty years. During this time his main care has been to always be with God: to do nothing, say nothing, and think nothing which might displease the Lord. He does this with no other motive than love for Him, and because the Lord deserves infinitely more than even this.

This brother is now so accustomed to that Divine Presence that he receives a continual nourishment from it at all times. For about thirty years now his soul has been filled with continual joy. Sometimes his joy is so

great that he is forced to moderate his expression of it.*
If sometimes this brother has been absent from the Divine
Presence a little too long (Which happens most when he
is engaged in his *outward* business), then before long
God makes Himself felt in that brother's soul and recalls
him! This brother answers the inward drawings of the
Lord with exact fidelity. He does so either by an evalu-
ation of his heart toward God, or by a meek and loving
look toward Him, or by such words as love forms upon
these occasions. As an example, he responds to the Lord,
"My God, behold me, wholly devoted to you. Lord,
make me according to Your heart."

Then something happens. He has a feeling that
the God of love, Who is satisfied with even such a few
words, again rests in the depth and center of his soul.
The experience of these things gives to our brother such
an assurance that God is there, always, deep within his
soul, that it renders him incapable of doubting it, no
matter what happens.

You can judge from this what contentment and
satisfaction our brother enjoys in continually finding this
great treasure within him. He no longer anxiously
searches for treasure. It is there, open before him; he is
free to take what he pleases of it.

This brothers sometimes complains of our blindness. He says that those of us who content ourselves
with so little of God are to be pitied. He has said that

God's treasure is like an infinite ocean, yet if even a little wave of
feeling, which lasts for only a moment, comes to us we are content.

---

*To prevent its appearing to be only outward

By such blindness we hinder God and stop the current of His graces. But when the Lord finds a soul permeated by His living faith, He is able to pour into that soul an abundance of His grace and favor. Such grace and favor flow into the soul like a torrent, which, having been forcibly stopped from its original course, once it has found a passage, spreads and flows again, unleashing its pent-up flow.

Yes, we often stop this torrent by the little value we set upon it. But let us stop it no more; let us enter our spirits and break down the bank which hinders it. Let us make way for grace; let us redeem the lost time, for perhaps we have only a little left. Death follows us closely; let us be prepared for him.

Let us turn within. Time is passing quickly and our very souls are at stake. I believe you have sought to respond to the Lord's Spirit. I commend you, for this is the one necessary thing in our lives. We must, nevertheless continue to work at it.

Why?

Because not to advance in the spiritual life is to go backward. Not to advance is to retreat. But those who feel the strong wind of the Holy Spirit go forward even in their sleep! And if the vessel of our soul is still tossed by the winds and storms, then let us awake the Lord who reposes inside. He will respond, and he will quickly calm the sea.

I have taken the liberty to impart to you these sentiments that you may compare them with your own. Please do so, because, if your own sentiments have cooled toward the Lord, this will help to inflame them again.

Let us both recall our first and original fervor to live in the Lord's presence. Let us both be encouraged by the example and sentiments of this brother who is so unknown in the world, but so well known by the Lord and so caressed by the Lord.

I pray for you. Do the same for me.

XV
Consecration

1685

Today I received two books in the mail from our dear sister. As you know she is about to take her vows as a nun. She asked for the prayers of those who are in your order and particularly for your prayers. I have the strong impression she is counting greatly on those prayers. Pray, do not disappoint her.

As you go to the Lord in her behalf, ask the Lord, no, beg Him, that she may make this consecration from only one view . . . that she is giving herself to Him because of His love alone. Further, pray that she resolve to be wholly and completely devoted to Him alone.

I am sending you one of these books, which deals with the practice of the presence of Christ. This subject, in my opinion, contains the whole spiritual life. It appears to me anyone who will practice dwelling

65

constantly in the Lord's presence will soon become spiritual.

Allow me to go a little further. If a Christian is to truly practice the presence of his Lord, and do so properly, then the heart of that Christian must be empty of all else. *All.* Why? Because God wills to possess that heart, and He wills to be the only possessor of that heart, and the only possession in that heart. He cannot be the only possessor of your heart unless it is empty of all else. He cannot put what He desires into a heart unless that heart has been left vacant for Him alone to refill it.

Do you know the highest kind of life we can experience? There is no other life in all the world as sweet and as delightful as the life lived in a continual walk with God. Even as I write such a statement I realize that the only ones who can comprehend it are those who have practiced and experienced that unbroken walk with the Lord.

Let me quickly add that I do not advise you to walk this way simply because it is "sweet and delightful!" It is not pleasure which we seek. Let this exercise be done from one motive alone: because we love Him. We walk with Him because it is His desire and His purpose that we walk with Him.

If I were a preacher, above everything else I would preach the practice of dwelling in the presence of Christ. If I had its ear, I would advise all the world to practice His presence; this is how necessary and how easy I think it to be.

Oh! If we but knew the need we have of God's

presence. If we could only see how greatly we need the Lord's assistance in everything. If we could really see how helpless we are without Him, we would never lose sight of Him, not even for a moment.

Dear sister, this *very* instant, make a resolution, a firm and holy resolution to never again willfully stray from Him. Stop now and agree with the Lord to live the rest of your days in His sacred presence. Then, out of love for Him, surrender all other pleasures.

Is this possible? Of course, if you believe it is. Set yourself to this heartily. If you perform this adventure as you should, you will soon see the effects.

I will assist you with my poor prayers.

XVI
Devoted Wholly to Him

I cannot imagine how a Christian can live a satisfied Christian experience without the practice of being in the presence of Christ. For my part, I keep myself retired with Him in the center of my soul as much as I can. While I am with Him I fear nothing. Even the slightest turning away from Him, on my part, is indefensible.

You asked if this practice is fatiguing to the body? It is not, but there is something to be said at this point. It is proper sometimes, even often, to deprive the body of many little pleasures, including pleasures that are pleasant and even lawful. God will not permit Christians who desire to be devoted wholly and entirely to Him to take other pleasures except the pleasure of Him alone. This is more than reasonable.

Please do not misunderstand. I am not suggesting that we put violent constraints upon ourselves. Not at

69

all, for we must serve the Lord in a holy freedom. Rather, we must do our business faithfully, without being troubled or disquieted, recalling our minds to God. Whenever we find our minds wandering from Him, we must recall them to His presence with tranquillity.

In order to do this you will find it necessary to put your whole trust in God, to lay aside all other cares. You will also find it necessary to lay aside some forms of devotion, even if they are good ones. Such devotions are only the means to the end. They were given to you to bring you to Christ's presence. Once you are in His presence, the forms are meaningless. When we are in His presence this *is* the end; it is therefore of no value to return to the means. Persevere to be with Him.

You may continue with Him in an exchange of love simply by an act of praise, or adoration, or just by desire. You may continue in His holy presence by an attitude of simple waiting, or by thanksgiving. Remain there by all the ways which your spirit can invent.

Do not be discouraged at the outset of this exercise. Your own nature may rebel at this holding and stillness before God. Do it violence; deny it. For instance, you may have the thought that this communion is a waste of valuable time. Pay that thought no attention. Go on with the Lord. Resolve to persevere before Him to the very death, regardless of any and all difficulties which arise.

I commend myself to the prayers of those who are in your order and to you in particular.

XVII
Some Practical Words

Let me express my feelings. You are now sixty-four; I am nearly eighty. Why not live — and die — with the Lord. It would be wonderful if you would just leave your present worldly affairs in the hands of your relatives and spend the rest of your life worshipping God.

The Lord does not really lay any great burden on us. He only wants you to recall Him to mind as often as possible, to pour out your adoration on Him, to pray for His grace. Offer Him your sorrows. Return from time to time to Him, and quietly, purely thank Him for the benefit He has given you in knowing Him. Thank Him, too, for the benefit He pours out upon you even in the midst of your troubles. The Lord asks you to let Him be the one who consoles you, just as often as you can find it in you to come to Him.

Lift your heart to the Lord at every meal, even when you have company. Any time you recall the Lord, no matter how faintly or how rarely, He finds it acceptable. You do not even need to speak loudly. He is very near to you when you are offering Him thanks.

Dear sister in Christ, you do not have to "go to church," to be in the presence of the Lord. You may come to Him by yourself. Learn to express your heart as you turn to the Lord within. Speak to Him. Speak with meekness, humility and love.

Anyone is capable of a very close and intimate dialogue with the Lord. It is true, some find it easier than others. But remember, the Lord knows that fact, too! So begin. Whether you are one who finds this easy or difficult is not important. Begin. He knows which category you are in! It just may be that He is only waiting for a resolution on your part to start. So make that resolution. Now!

Be daring. None of us have a long time to live. Again, what years we have, let us live them with God. If there is any suffering, it will be sweet, even pleasant, while we are with *Him.* And sister, without *Him* the greatest pleasure you could ever have would be but anguish.

Oh, may He be blessed for all. Amen.

A last word. Begin now to accustom yourself, little by little, to worshipping Him. Ask Him for grace. Offer Him your whole heart. Over and again, in the midst of business, every moment if you can, just offer Him your heart. (This can be done without a single utterance escaping you. Or, you can express yourself quietly, yet audibly, by whispering your love to Him.) Do not get weighted down with a lot of rules, or forms, or ways;

act with faith — just come. But come in an attitude of love and deep humility.

My poor prayers go with you.

XVIII
Beyond Any Method

A few days ago I was talking to a brother of piety. He told me that the spiritual life was a life of peace which was arrived at in three steps. He said there is first fear; after that, fear is changed to hope of eternal life; finally there is a consummation, that of pure love. He said each of these three states is a different stage which eventually brings one to "that blessed consummation."

I have never followed this method. On the contrary, it was because I had myself been so discouraged by such methods that, when I finally came to the Lord, I decided just to give myself up to Him. This gift of myself was the best satisfaction I could hope to make for my sins. I realized that only out of pure love for Him could I renounce all the other concerns and interests of the world.

During my early years of seeking God I did use methods. I would set aside specific times to devote my thoughts to death, judgment, heaven, hell or my sins. I did this for years. But during the rest of the day I began doing something else. I spent the rest of my time, even in the midst of my business, carefully turning my mind to the presence of God. I always considered that His presence was with me, even *in* me!

Finally I even gave up using those set times of prayer for any type of methodical devotion which was a great delight and comfort to me. I began to use my regular times of devotion in the same way I did the rest of my time, in fixing my mind on the presence of God. This new practice revealed to me even more of the worth of my Lord. Faith alone, not a method, and certainly not fear, was able to satisfy me in coming to Him.

That was my beginning.

The next ten years were very hard, and I suffered a great deal. I was afraid I was not as devoted to God as I wanted to be; my past sins were always present in my mind; and there was the problem of the undeserved favors which God bestowed upon me! These matters were the source of my sufferings.

During this period I often fell, yet just as often I rose again. Sometimes it seemed that all creation, reason and even the Lord Himself were against me . . . and faith alone was for me. I was troubled with the thought that perhaps it was pure presumption on my part to believe I had received favor and mercy from God, and that this presumption only pretended to have taken me to a point that others arrived at only after going through many difficult stages. On occasion I even thought perhaps my simple touch with God was just a willful delusion on my part, and that I didn't even have salvation!

Amazingly, all those doubts and fears did not diminish my trust in God but rather served to increase my faith. Finally, I came to the realization that I should put aside all the thoughts which brought about these times of trouble and unrest. Immediately I found myself changed. My soul, which had been so troubled, then felt a profound sense of inward peace and rest.

Ever since that time I have walked before God in simple faith. I have walked there with humility and love. Now I have but one thing to do: to apply myself diligently to being in God's presence, and to do nothing and say nothing that would displease Him. I hope that when I have done what I can, He will do with me whatever He pleases.

Many years have passed since that time. I have no pain and no doubt in my present state, because I have no will but God's. To that will I am so submissive that I would not take up a straw from the ground against His order, nor would I pick it up out of any other motive than purely that of love for Him.

I have given up *all forms* of devotion and set prayers other than those to which my state obliges me. My only business now is to persevere in His holy presence. I do so by a simple and loving attention to the Lord. Then I have the experience of the actual presence of God. To use another term I will call it a *secret* conversation between my soul and the Lord.

A question frequently asked me is, "What do you do about your mind wandering off on other things?"

This does happen, sometimes of necessity, sometimes out of weakness. But the Lord soon recalls me. I am recalled by an inward emotion or an inward sense so charming and delightful that I am at a loss as to know exactly how to describe it.

Do not be impressed with me because of what I am telling you. You are well aware of my weaknesses, so keep them in mind. I am utterly unworthy and ungrateful of the great favor the Lord has turned upon me.

My set times for prayer are exactly like the rest of the day to me. They are but a continuation of the same exercise of being in God's presence. Sometimes I see myself as a stone before the carver, ready to be made a statue. I present myself to God desiring Him to form His own perfect image in my soul and to make me entirely like Himself. At other times while praying, I feel my whole spirit and soul lifted up, with no effort on my part at all, to the very center and being of God.

Some people have said that this state is nothing but inactivity, delusion and self-love on my part. I agree that it is a holy inactivity, and it would be a happy self-love if the soul were capable of self-love in that state. But actually the very reverse is true. When the soul is at rest in God it does not follow its usual selfish behavior; its love is only for God.

I cannot bear, either, to regard this as "delusion." When my inner man is in the Lord's presence, enjoying Him, it desires nothing except the Lord! If this is a delusion, then it is up to God to remedy it.

Lord, do with me as You please. I desire only you, and to be wholly devoted to you.

78

XIX
Advice to a Soldier

October 12, 1688

I read your letter about your son, the problem he faces in the military, his accident and your concern.

We have a God who is infinitely gracious and knows all about our wants. I always thought that He would reduce you to extremity, for the Lord comes to us in just these ways, in His time, and when we least expect it.

Now, what should be your attitude? How do you react to the Lord when He brings things like this upon you? You should hope in Him now more than ever. Thank Him, as I am thanking Him, for the favors He does give you. What favors? For the fortitude and patience He is giving you during your affliction. They are a clear proof that He is caring for you. Comfort yourself then, *through* Him, and thank Him for everything.

I admit I admire the bravery of your son. God gave

him a good disposition and a good will. But I am afraid there is still a little of the world in him and a great deal of youth. I hope the affliction which the Lord sent him will turn out to be good medicine to him. I hope that because of this, he will pause and take stock of himself. It is the kind of accident which should cause him to put all his trust in a Lord who is, in fact, accompanying him wherever he goes.

But how can he be aware of a God who is always with him? It is really quite simple. Let him just think of the Lord as often as he can — especially, of course, in the face of danger.

Just a little lifting up of the heart to God is enough. A little remembrance of the Lord, one act of inward worship, though upon a march or with a sword in hand, will be fully accepted by the Lord. Far from lessening a soldier's courage in occasions of danger, these brief moments in the Lord's presence will rather fortify him.

Therefore let this young man set his mind upon God as often as he can. He can accustom himself to this simple exercise, this small but holy exercise, little by little. No one will even notice. And *nothing* is easier than to repeat these little internal adorations intermittently, all through the day.

I trust God will assist him, and you.

XX
Recalling
the Wandering Mind

Yours is not an unusual experience. Nearly everyone has problems with wandering thoughts. The mind is a true rover. But since the will is master of all our other faculties, it can recall the mind and carry our thoughts to God.

When I first began, my mind was also undisciplined. Because of this lack, my first efforts at devotion were hampered by the wandering and dissipation of my mind. Such habits are difficult to overcome. They even draw us away from the Lord and to the earth against our very will.

I believe one remedy for this is to confess our faults and to humble ourselves before God. I do not advise you to use a lot of words in these prayers. Many words and long discourses are just opportunities for your mind to wander.

Do this instead. Hold yourself before the Lord.

Remain there as a poor man sitting at a rich man's gate: waiting. Let it be your business to keep your mind in the presence of the Lord.

If your mind sometimes wanders or withdraws from the Lord, do not be upset or disquieted. Trouble and disquiet serve more to distract the mind further from God than to recollect it. The will must bring the mind back in tranquillity. If you persevere in this manner, the Lord will have pity on you.

One way to recollect the mind easily in the time of prayer, and to preserve it more in tranquillity, is *not* to let it wander too far at other times. Keep it strictly in the presence of God throughout each day. Become accustomed to recalling your mind to the Lord often. As you do this more and more you will find it easy to keep your mind calm in times of prayer and to recall it when it wanders.

Let us set about this seriously, and let us pray for each other.

XXI
The All-Inclusive
Solution

From your letter I see that your friend is full of good will toward the Lord, but she wishes to advance even faster than grace. A Christian simply cannot become holy all at once, no matter how much he perseveres, and no matter what experiences he can claim. I recommend your friend to your care. We ought to help one another with encouragement, and yet more by our good examples.

As often as possible we should recall that our only business in this life is to please God, and that all else besides the Lord is folly and vanity.

You and I have both lived a monastic life many years. Have we employed those years in loving God? After all, it was by His mercy we were called and chosen. And for what purpose? To love Him!

When I realize, on the one hand, the great favors

which God has poured out upon me, and is still incessantly pouring upon me, and then, on the other hand, look at the poor use I have made of such mercy and favor and the small advance my life has made toward perfection, I am sometimes filled with shame. But, praise His name, by His mercy He has given us both still a little more time. So let us begin in earnest with Him. Dear sister, repair the lost time. Return, with full assurance, to the very One who authored mercy and created grace. Return to your Father who always, at any time, is so utterly willing to receive you. More: He will receive you with the deepest affections.

Out of an active, overflowing love let us renounce all that is not Him. He certainly deserves this and more. Let us think on Him perpetually. Let us both put absolutely *all* our trust in Him. I have no doubt but that we will soon see the effects of this. It might appear we have lost all else but Christ; but oh, to receive the abundance of His grace, that is enough! By the abundance of that grace we can do all things. Without it we can do nothing but sin.

There is no way to escape the dangers which abound in life without the actual and continual help of the presence of God. Let us, then, pray to Him for it continually.

And how can we pray to Him without being *with* Him? And how can we be with Him without thinking of Him often? And how can we think of Him often without forming the holy habit of being in His presence?

You may tell me that I am always saying the same thing. It is true, for this is the best and easiest method I know. In it is the resolution to all other spiritual problems. And since I know of no other method, I advise all the world to follow this one.

Let me put it this way: before we can *love,* we must *know.* We must *know* someone before we can *love* him. How shall we keep our "first love" for the Lord? By constantly knowing Him better!

Then how shall we know the Lord? We must often turn to Him, think of Him, behold Him. *Then* our hearts will be found with our treasure.

This is an argument which well deserves your consideration!

XXII
Friend Suffering,
Friend Pain

Suffering is always painful, either to your body or to your soul. Yet though I know you are suffering, I am not praying that you will be delivered from your pain. Nonetheless, I do pray. I earnestly ask God to give you strength and patience to bear your pain as long as it pleases Him.

God has fastened you to a cross. Now, can you do this? Find your comfort in the very One who holds you fastened to that cross. He will loose you when He sees fit. Seek the Lord as your strength, the strength to endure as much and as long as He has measured out for you. Happy are those who suffer with Him.

Men who are in the world cannot understand this truth. That is no wonder. They do not suffer as Christians. They are in a different world from Christians; therefore, they consider sickness as something gone wrong in nature, and not as a favor from God. In looking at pain from their view, there is nothing in it but grief and distress. But if we consider sickness to be a gift from the hand of God, an expression of His mercy and an instrument which He uses to bring us to complete salvation, *then* suffering is something very sweet. It is reasonable and even comforting. God, in some sense, is even nearer to you when you are sick.

Rely upon no other physician; for according to my understanding, the Lord reserves the cure to Himself. He will remedy your sickness in His time. Therefore, put all your trust in Him and you will soon discover the effect on your recovery. We often retard our recovery by putting a greater confidence in the medical world than in God.

It has been my observation that even the medicine we take succeeds only as far as the Lord permits. When the pain comes from God, then God alone can take the pain away. The Lord often sends diseases to the body in order to cure the disease of the soul.

Comfort yourself with the sovereign Physician, who is the healer of both body and soul.

Dear friend, be content with the condition God has put you in. However happy you may think me, I envy you. Pains and suffering would be a paradise to me as long as the Lord was with me; and the greatest pleasures of this earth would be hell to me if I had to taste them without Him.

All the comfort I need can be found in the privilege of suffering just because it is His desire that I suffer.

In a little time, I will go to God. What comforts me in this life is that I now see my Lord by faith. In seeing

Him by faith I actually see so well I sometimes say, "I believe no more! I see!"

I can *feel* that which faith teaches; I can sense what faith sees. This of course, works great assurance in me. In that assurance and in that practice of faith, I will live and die with Him.

So continue always with God. To be with Him is really your only support and your only comfort during affliction.

I shall beseech my Lord to be with you.

XXIII
His Numberless Ways

If we were all completely accustomed to being constantly in the presence of Christ, all our disease would be much alleviated by that presence. The Lord does *very* often allow us to suffer a little.* He does so for two reasons: to purify the soul and to oblige us to *continue* in His presence (or, if it is our need, to turn us — through suffering — back into His presence).

What shall you do in your present straits? Constantly, incessantly offer your pains to the Lord. Ask Him for strength to endure the pain. But above all else, get into the habit of entertaining yourself with God. Forget Him the very least you can.

During your pain, just adore Him. From time to

---

*Two of the most traumatic experiences a Christian can have are (1) long periods of intense pain and suffering and (2) the loss of the presence of God. Brother Lawrence touches both of these depths in this letter.

time offer yourself to Him. In the very height of your suffering just beseech Him, very humbly and very affectionately — let me repeat, affectionately — that He will conform you to His will.

I shall be what aid I can to you with my prayers.

God seems to have endless ways of drawing us to Himself. Perhaps His most unusual way is to hide Himself from you. What can we do when we can no longer find the Lord? The key is found in the word *faith.* Faith is the one thing, perhaps the only thing, which will not fail you in such a time. Let faith be your support. The very foundation of your confidence must be your faith. At a time like that, when God seems to have forsaken you, you must exercise your faith in Him.

You ask about me. I am always happy. The whole world suffers, and here am I, the one person who deserves the severest discipline, feeling joys so continual and so great that I can scarce contain them!

I would willingly ask God for a part of your suffering, yet I know that I am so weak that if the Lord left me one moment to myself I would be the most wretched man alive. But, I cannot even consider that He could ever leave me alone. You see, faith gives me just as strong a conviction as the *senses* ever could that He never forsakes us.

Yes, I sense His presence continually. But if I should lose that sense, my faith that He is with me would be as strong as the sense had been.

Have but one fear: fear to leave Him. Be always with Him. Let us live in His presence. Let us die in His presence.

XXIV
Response to Pain

I am in pain to see you suffer so long. What gives me some ease is that your suffering is proof of God's love for you. When you really see your suffering from that view, you can bear your pains more easily.

As I said before, it is my own feeling you should quit taking the medicine and resign yourself entirely to the sovereignty and the providence of God.

Perhaps He is waiting just for that resignation and trust in Him. Consider my words. After all, despite your anxiety and your efforts to get well, the medical world has been completely unsuccessful in helping you; instead the disease has increased. Would it be so difficult to abandon yourself into His hands and expect all from Him?

In my last letter I said to you that the Lord sometimes permits diseases of the body so that problems within the soul can be cured. Have courage; take this limitation and turn it to opportunity.

Come to the Lord, ask Him not to deliver you from your pain, but ask Him for strength to bear this thing. Ask Him to give you a deep, strong love for Him. Ask Him to give you everything that would please Him. Ask Him to give you what He will and to do with you what He wishes, as long as He pleases.

A prayer like that is a little difficult to pray. Such a prayer is against the nature of the soul, but it is one very acceptable to God. It is a sweet prayer of resignation to those who love the Lord. Love sweetens pains. And when a Christian loves God, he can suffer for His sake, joyfully and courageously.

I beseech you to do just that. Comfort yourself with the Lord. He is the *only* Physician who can meet all our needs. The Lord Jesus is the Comforter of the ill, the Father of the afflicted. He is always ready to help you; but His help comes according to the way He desires and not the way you desire.

He loves you. He loves you infinitely more than you can imagine. So what should you do? Love Him. Then, seek to obtain your comfort from Him and Him alone.

I trust you will be able to receive these words. Adieu.

I will help you with my prayers even though they are very poor, and I shall always be yours in the Lord.

XXV
Paradise Redefined

January 22, 1691

I praise the Lord that He has relieved you a little, just as you desired.

Many times I have been at the point of death, and I have never been so content as at that time. Consequently, I did not pray for relief. Rather, I asked the Lord for strength to suffer with courage, humility and love.

Oh, how sweet it is to suffer with God! However great the sufferings may be, receive them all with *love*. Dear Christian friend, it is paradise to suffer with the Lord. It is paradise to be with Him under *any* conditions! It is possible for us to live in the very sense of the Lord's presence, under even the most difficult circumstances.

If you and I are going to enjoy the peace of paradise during this life we must become accustomed to a familiar, humble and very affectionate conversation with the Lord Jesus. You must stop your spirit from wandering from the Lord no matter what the circumstances are. You must make your heart a spiritual temple, a temple where you can go to adore Him incessantly.

XXVI
Infinite Riches

How happy we would be if we could all find that "Treasure" which the Gospel speaks of. All else would be as nothing to us. How infinite that treasure is. The more one searches through it, the more he finds. The more he toils in it, the greater the riches he gains. So let us not grow weary and stop until we have found that treasure and fully explored it.

What my end will be and what I shall become, I do not know. But I am to the point that a peace of soul and rest of spirit descend upon me even when I am asleep. To be without this sense, this constant sense of peace, would be suffering indeed; but with peace in my inner being I believe I could find consolation even in purgatory.

No, I do not know what God purposes with me, nor what is in store for me. But I am in a calm so great that I fear nothing. What could I fear? I am with Him. And there, with Him, in His presence, is where I keep myself all I can.

May all things praise Him.

XXVII
Think on Him Often

I am pleased with the trust you have in God; I also hope He will increase that trust which has now begun growing in you.

There is no way for you to have too much trust in so good and so faithful a friend as Jesus Christ, for He will never fail you, not in this world or in the next.

Concerning the brother you asked me to write: if he takes advantage of the loss of the one so dear to him, if he puts all his confidence in God, the Lord will soon give him another friend, a friend more powerful and more inclined to serve him. The Lord disposes of hearts as He pleases. Perhaps our brother was too attached to the one he lost. Of course we ought to love our friends, but we must love them without encroaching upon the love due to the Lord. Our love to Him comes first.

Are you keeping in mind what I recommended to you? Think often of God; do so by day and by night, in your business and even during diversions. The Lord is always near you. He is with you. For your part, never leave Him alone. It would be rude, don't you think, to leave a friend all alone who had come to visit? Why is it then, that God is so often neglected?

Do not forget the Lord. Think on Him often; adore Him continually. Live and die with Him. This is the glorious employment of a Christian. This is our profession as Christians. If we do not already do this, then we must learn to do it.

I will seek to aid you with my prayers.

XXVIII
Always in His Presence

Once Brother Lawrence was questioned by one of his society, a man to whom he was obliged to answer, concerning what means he had used to attain such a habitual sense of God. He told the superior that since first coming to the monastery he had considered God to be the end of all his thoughts and desires. He explained that he considered God the mark to which all thoughts and desires should tend and in which they should all terminate.

In the beginning of his novitiate he spent the hours appointed for prayer in thinking of God. The purpose of this was to convince his mind and to impress deeply upon his heart the divine existence. This was done by devout sentiments and by submission to the lights of faith rather than by studied reason and elaborate meditations. By this short and sure method he was able to exercise himself in the love and knowledge of God. He had resolved to use his inmost endeavors to live in a continual sense of the Lord's presence and, if possible, never to forget Him.

When he had filled his mind, through prayer, with great sentiments of divine Being, he went to his appointed work in the kitchen (he was a cook in the society). There he first considered carefully the things that his office required, when and how each thing was to be done. He then spent all the intervals of his time, and before and after his work, in prayer.

When he began his business he said to God, with a filial trust in Him: "Oh my God, since You are with me, and I must now, in obedience to Your commands, apply my mind to these outward things, I ask You to grant me the grace to continue in Your presence. To this end make me prosper through Your assistance. Receive all my works, and possess all my affections."

He proceeded in his work each day, continuing his familiar conversation with his Maker, imploring the Lord for His grace, and offering to the Lord all his actions.

When Brother Lawrence had finished, he examined how he had discharged his duties. If he found he had done well, he returned thanks to God; if he found otherwise, he asked pardon, and without being discouraged he set his mind right again. He then continued his exercise of the presence of God as if he had never deviated from it. Brother Lawrence commented, "Thus, by rising after my falls, and by frequently renewing my acts of faith and love, I have come to a state wherein it would be as difficult for me not to think of

102

God as it was at first to accustom myself to think of Him."

As Brother Lawrence found such an advantage in walking in the presence of God, it was natural for him to recommend it earnestly to others. But his example was a stronger inducement than any arguments he could ever have proposed. His very countenance was edifying, with such a sweet and calm devotion appearing in it as could not but affect its beholders. It was observed that in the greatest hurry of business in the kitchen, he still preserved his recollection and heavenly-mindedness. He was neither hasty nor loitering, but did each thing in its season, with an even, uninterrupted composure and tranquillity of spirit. "The time of business," said he, "does not differ with me from the time of prayer; and in the noise and clatter of my kitchen, while several persons are at the same time calling for different things, I possess God in as great a tranquillity as if I were upon my knees at the blessed sacrament."

XXIX
Au Revoir

February 6, 1691

The Lord knows best what is needful for us. What He does, He does for our good. If we *really* knew just how much He loves us, we would always be willing to receive anything from His hand. We would receive the bitter or the sweet without distinction.

Anything, yes everything, would please us just because it came from Him.

The worst possible afflictions and suffering appear intolerable *only* when seen in the wrong light. When we see such things as dispensed by the hand of God, when we know that it is our own loving Father who abases us and distresses us, then our sufferings lose their bitterness. Our mourning becomes all joy.

Let all your employment be to know God. The more you actually *know* Him the more you will desire to know Him. Since knowledge is a measurement of love, the

105

deeper and more intimate you are with Him, the greater will be your love for Him. And if our love for the Lord is great, then we will love Him as much during grief as in joy.

I am sure you know that most people's love for the Lord stops at a very shallow stage. Most love God for the tangible things He gives them. They love Him because of His favor to them. You must not stop on such a level, no matter how rich His mercies have been to you. Many outward blessings can never bring you as close to God as can one simple act of faith.

So seek Him often by faith.

Oh, dear friend, the Lord is not outside of you, pouring down favors. The Lord is within you. Seek Him there, within . . . and no where else.

Let the Lord be the one, the only, love of your life. If we do love Him alone, are we not rude if we busy ourselves with trifles, trifles which do not please Him and some which may even offend Him? Be wise and fear such trifles. They will one day cost us dearly.

Dear friend, would you now begin, today, to be devoted to the Lord, in earnest? Cast everything else out of your heart. He would possess it alone. Beg of Him that favor.

Do what you can, and soon you will see that change wrought in you which you are seeking.

I cannot thank Him enough for the relief He has given you.

I hope, by His mercy, for the privilege of seeing Him face to face within a few days.

Let us pray for one another.

Brother Lawrence was confined to bed two days after writing this last letter, and died the same week. Surely he recognized his Lord very quickly, for while he had been bound by his earthly body his eyes of faith rarely looked anywhere but upon the Lord.

Epilogue

Since the first printing of this book, and the more recent *Experiencing the Depths of Jesus Christ,* we have received a number of touching letters from Christians around the country. There is no question: there are a vast number of Christians out there who are not content. Today's Christianity does not satisfy, is not deep enough; its formulas are all wanting.

We are publishing these books to help satisfy the hunger that is so widespread. But we also want to tell you something. It is this: God did not give you the presence of Christ just to make you blissfully happy all your life. He saved you to put you into His kingdom. And, in the first century at least, all believers had a vital part in the daily and very practical experience of that kingdom. They called it the body of Christ. We call it the church.

Whatever it is, it is basic, practical, real. And whatever it is — though it has many inferior imitations (such as "community," "going to church on Sunday," etc.) — church life is an experience unknown to Christians today.

Here is my plea. In all of your seeking to know Christ in a real and deep way, don't forget to seek to know Him as they did in the first century. They *all* knew Him in the context of practical church life.

May you find Him. But may you also find that further experience of knowing Him in the daily experience of the body of Christ.

G. E.

Books you might like to read

◆ Radical books for radical readers

BEYOND RADICAL

A simple, historical introduction into how we got all of our present-day Christian practices.

You will be thunderstruck to discover that there is really *nothing* we are doing today in our church practice that came directly out of man's determination to be scriptural. Virtually everything we do came into being sometime during church history, after the New Testament. We have spent the rest of our time trying to bend the Scripture to justify the practice.

WHEN THE CHURCH WAS LED *ONLY* BY LAYMEN

The word *elder* appears in the New Testament seventeen times, the word *pastor* appears only once (and nobody knows what that word had reference to, because there is no place in the first-century story in which he is clearly seen).

But there are over one hundred and thirty references from the day of Pentecost forward that refer to either "brothers" or "brothers and the sisters" (Greek: *Adolphus*). *These* were the people who were leading the church. There are only two major players, from a human viewpoint, upon the first-century stage. They are the church planters and God's people—the brothers and the sisters. Everything else is a footnote.

OVERLOOKED CHRISTIANITY

What is the view of the Trinity on these three critical aspects of faith:

1. How to live the Christian life
2. What is "church" really supposed to look like
3. How are workers—specifically *church* planters—supposed to be trained

Revolutionary, radical and arresting! These are the words which best describe this one-of-a-kind book!

Overlooked Christianity makes a great companion book to *Rethinking Elders* and gives clear answers about *what to do* in the practice of our Christian life!

AN OPEN LETTER TO
HOUSE CHURCH LEADERS

A simple statement on what a more primitive expression of the Christian faith should be centering on.

◆ Books which show what the Christian faith was like "first-century style"

REVOLUTION, the Story of the Early Church
THE SILAS DIARY
THE TITUS DIARY
THE TIMOTHY DIARY
THE PRISCILLA DIARY
THE GAIUS DIARY

The story! Perhaps the best way we will ever understand what it was like from the day of Pentecost in 30 A.D. until the close of the first century is simply to know the story. Allow yourself to be treated to, and enthralled by, that story. (Warning: Knowing the story will change your life forever.) You will find that story in every detail, with nothing missing, in these *six* books.

◆ Books which glorify Jesus Christ

THE DIVINE ROMANCE
A book of awe, wonder and beauty.

THE STORY OF MY LIFE AS TOLD BY
JESUS CHRIST
Matthew, Mark, Luke and John combined into one complete gospel written in first-person singular.

ACTS IN FIRST-PERSON
Beginning with Acts 1, Peter tells the story of Acts through chapter 11. Then Barnabas, speaking in first person, tells the story of Acts from chapter 13 to chapter 15. You then hear Silas, Timothy and Luke continue the story all the way through, ending with chapter 28.

THE CHRONICLES OF THE DOOR
The record of heaven as told in;
THE BEGINNING
THE ESCAPE
THE BIRTH
THE TRIUMPH
(the resurrection)
THE RETURN

◆ Books which show you how to experience Christ

The following books serve as an introduction to the Deeper Christian Life:

LIVING BY THE HIGHEST LIFE
THE SECRET TO THE CHRISTIAN LIFE
THE INWARD JOURNEY

◆ Books that heal

Here are books that have been used all over the world, and in many languages, to heal Christians from the deep, deep pains they experience as they go through life. Some were written for Christians who have been damaged by their churches and damaged by other Christians. Others are books which help you understand the ways of God as they are now working in your life. All of these books are known and loved around the world.

A TALE OF THREE KINGS

A study in brokenness based on the story of Saul, David and Absalom.

THE PRISONER IN THE THIRD CELL

A study in the mysteries of God's ways, especially when He works contrary to all your understanding and expectations of Him.

CRUCIFIED BY CHRISTIANS

Healing for Christians who have been crucified by other Christians.

LETTERS TO A DEVASTATED CHRISTIAN

This book explores different techniques practiced by Christian groups who demand extreme submission and passivity from their members. It faces the difficult task of dealing with bitterness and resentment and rebuilding of faith and trust.

Contact SeedSowers Publishing House for a catalog of these and other books, including great classics from the past on the deeper Christian life, as well as new publications that will be appearing annually.

SeedSowers
PO Box 285
Sargent, GA 30275
800-228-2665
www.seedsowers.com

Prices as of 20

REVOLUTIONARY BOOKS ON CHURCH LIFE

The House Church Movement (Begier, Richey, Vasiliades, Viola)... 9.
How to Meet In Homes *(Edwards)*.. 10.
An Open Letter to House Church Leaders *(Edwards)*......................4.
When the Church Was Led *Only* by Laymen *(Edwards)*.................. 4.
Beyond Radical *(Edwards)*... 5.
Rethinking Elders *(Edwards)*.. 9.
Revolution, The Story of the Early Church *(Edwards)*......8.
The Silas Diary *(Edwards)*.. 9.
The Titus Diary *(Edwards)*... 8.
The Timothy Diary *(Edwards)*.. 9.
The Priscilla Diary *(Edwards)* .... 9.
Overlooked Christianity *(Edwards)*... 14.

AN INTRODUCTION TO THE DEEPER CHRISTIAN LIFE
Living by the Highest Life *(Edwards)*.. 8.
The Secret to the Christian Life *(Edwards)*.....................8.
The Inward Journey *(Edwards)*... 8.

CLASSICS ON THE DEEPER CHRISTIAN LIFE
Experiencing the Depths of Jesus Christ *(Guyon)*............................ 8.
Practicing His Presence *(Lawrence/Laubach)*................................... 8.
The Spiritual Guide *(Molinos)*.. 8.
Song of the Bride *(Guyon)*... 9.
Union With God *(Guyon)*... 8.
The Seeking Heart *(Fenelon)*... 9.
Intimacy with Christ *(Guyon)* .... 14.
Spiritual Torrents *(Guyon)*... 14.
The Ultimate Intention *(Fromke)*... 11.0

IN A CLASS BY THEMSELVES
The Divine Romance *(Edwards)*.. 8.
The Story of My Life as told by Jesus Christ (Four gospels blended).....14.
Acts in First-Person.. 9.

THE CHRONICLES OF THE DOOR *(Edwards)*
The Beginning... 8.
The Escape... 8.9
The Birth.. 8.
The Triumph... 8.
The Return.. 8.9

IE WORKS OF T. AUSTIN-SPARKS

The Centrality of Jesus Christ...................................... 19.95
The House of God... 29.95
Ministry... 29.95
Service... 19.95

OMFORT AND HEALING

A Tale of Three Kings *(Edwards)*............................... 8.95
The Prisoner in the Third Cell *(Edwards)*.................. 7.95
Letters to a Devastated Christian *(Edwards)*............. 5.95
Healing for those who have been Crucified by Christians *(Edwards)*....... 8.95
Dear Lillian *(Edwards)*... 5.95

THER BOOKS ON CHURCH LIFE

Climb the Highest Mountain *(Edwards)*..................... 9.95
The Torch of the Testimony *(Kennedy)*..................... 14.95
The Passing of the Torch *(Chen)*................................ 9.95
Going to Church in the First Century *(Banks)*........... 5.95
When the Church was Young *(Loosley)*..................... 14.95
Church Unity *(Litzman, Nee, Edwards)*..................... 14.95
Let's Return to Christian Unity *(Kurosaki)*................ 14.95

HRISTIAN LIVING

Final Steps in Christian Maturity *(Guyon)*................ 12.95
The Key to Triumphant Living *(Taylor)*..................... 9.95
Turkeys and Eagles *(Lord)*... 8.95
Beholding and Becoming *(Coulter)*........................... 8.95
Life's Ultimate Privilege *(Fromke)*........................... 7.00
Unto Full Stature *(Fromke)*....................................... 7.00
All and Only *(Kilpatrick)*... 7.95
Adoration *(Kilpatrick)* 8.95
Release of the Spirit *(Nee)* 5.00
Bone of His Bone *(Huegel)* 8.95
Christ as All in All *(Haller)* 9.95

Please write or call for our current catalog:

 SeedSowers
P.O. Box 285
Sargent, GA 30275
800-228-2665
www.seedsowers.com
e-mail: books@seedsowers.com